Easy Dumpling Cookbook

50 Delicious Dumpling Recipes

By
BookSumo Press

Published by
http://www.booksumo.com

Table of Contents

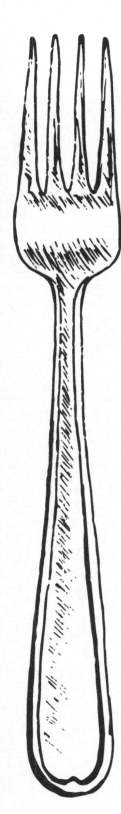

Creamy Chicken Thighs Soup with Dumplings 26

Orangy Apple Dumplings 27

Creamy Corn and Chicken Dumplings Stew 28

Cinnamon Apple Dumplings 29

Chicken Breasts Stew with Milk Dumplings 30

Rotisserie Chicken Stew with Dill Dumplings 31

Hearty Creamy Chicken Soup with Dumplings 32

Twice Stuffed Dumplings 33

Turkey Stew with Buttermilk Dumplings 35

Creamy Allspice Chicken Stew with Dumplings 36

Caramelized Apple Dumplings 37

Thanksgiving Stew with Stuffing Dumplings 38

Maple Blueberry and Apple Dumplings 40

Jarlsberg's Dumplings Casserole 41

French Milk Dumplings 42

Asian Stuffed Shrimp Dumplings 43

Prune Stuffed Potato Dumplings 44

Vanilla Raisins Dumplings 46

Seafood Stuffed Dumplings 47

Creamy Paprika Chicken with Parsley Dumplings 48

Chili Dumpling Sauce 49

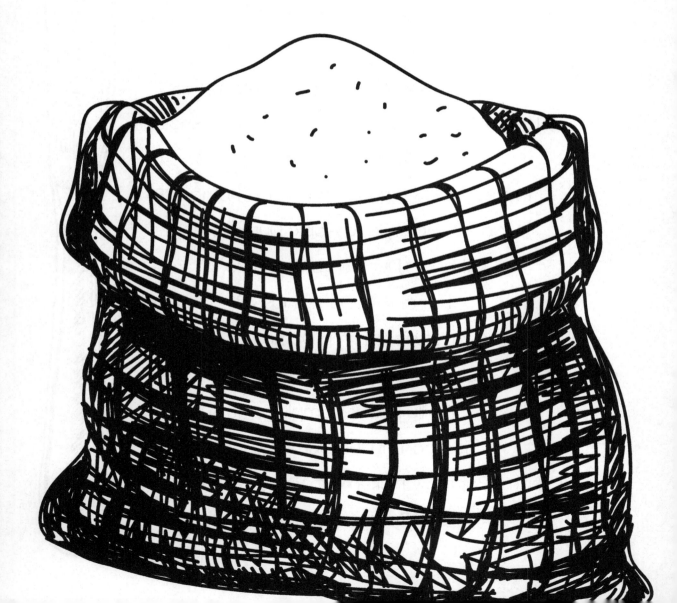

Classic
Milk Dumplings

Prep Time: 5 mins
Total Time: 20 mins

Servings per Recipe: 6
Calories	105 kcal
Fat	2.4 g
Carbohydrates	18g
Protein	2.8 g
Cholesterol	2 mg
Sodium	386 mg

Ingredients

1 C. all-purpose flour
2 tsp baking powder
1 tsp white sugar
1/2 tsp salt
1 tbsp margarine

1/2 C. milk

Directions

1. Get a large mixing bowl: Combine in it the flour, baking powder, sugar, and salt. Mix them well. Slice the butter and add it the mix. Mix them until the flour mix become crumbled.
2. Add the milk and mix them until you get a smooth and soft dough. Spoon the dough into your stew that is boiling. Put on the lid and cook it for 16 min.
3. Serve your dumplings stew warm.
4. Enjoy.

CHICKEN
Flavored
Dumplings

Prep Time: 20 mins
Total Time: 1 hr

Servings per Recipe: 7	
Calories	226 kcal
Fat	10.5 g
Carbohydrates	28.4g
Protein	4.3 g
Cholesterol	1 mg
Sodium	479 mg

Ingredients

2 C. all-purpose flour
2 tsp baking powder
1 tsp salt
1/3 C. shortening
1/2 C. milk

2 (14.5 oz) cans chicken broth

Directions

1. Get a large mixing bowl: Combine in it the flour with baking powder and salt. Slice the shortening into cubes and add it to the mix with milk.
2. Mix them well until they make a soft dough. Spread the dough on a floured surface until it becomes 1/8 inch thick then cut it into the shape you desire.
3. Place a soup pot over medium heat and bring the stock in it to a boil. Lower the dumplings into the stock and put on the lid. Cook them for 9 min then serve them warm hot.
4. Enjoy.

Vanilla
and Buttermilk Biscuits Dumplings

🥣 Prep Time: 15 mins
🕐 Total Time: 55 mins

Servings per Recipe: 10	
Calories	275 kcal
Fat	13.9 g
Carbohydrates	36 g
Protein	2.6 g
Cholesterol	25 mg
Sodium	408 mg

Ingredients

1 (12 oz) can refrigerated buttermilk biscuit dough
2 C. chopped fresh rhubarb
1 C. white sugar
1 C. water

1/2 C. butter, melted
1 1/4 tsp vanilla extract
1/4 tsp ground cinnamon, or to taste

Directions

1. Before you do anything preheat the oven to 350 F.
2. Place the biscuits in a floured surface and flatten each one of them until they become 3 inches circled thick each.
3. In the middle of each biscuit place 1 tbsp of rhubarb. Pull the dough on top it to the middle to cover the rhubarb and pinch it to seal it.
4. Transfer the stuffed dumplings into a greased baking pan with their sealed side facing down.
5. Get a mixing bowl: Whisk in it the sugar, water, butter and vanilla. Drizzle the mix all over the dumplings and top them with cinnamon.
6. Cook them in the oven for 48 min until they become golden then serve them warm.
7. Enjoy.

FRUITY
Stuffed Potato Dumpling

 Prep Time: 1 hr 30 mins

Total Time: 2 hrs 15 mins

Servings per Recipe: 16

Calories	231 kcal
Fat	4 g
Carbohydrates	44.6g
Protein	5.3 g
Cholesterol	19 mg
Sodium	80 mg

Ingredients

3 tbsp butter
1 C. dry bread crumbs
4 large russet potatoes, peeled
1 tbsp butter
2 C. all-purpose flour
1 egg
1 pinch salt

16 Italian prune plums, pitted and left whole
16 tsp white sugar, divided

Directions

1. Place a large pan over medium heat. Add 3 tbsp of butter to it and heat until it melts. Add the breadcrumbs and cook them for 2 min 30 sec. Drain it and place it aside.
2. Bring a salted pot of water to a boil. Cook in it the potato until it becomes soft. Remove it from the water and place it aside to lose heat slightly and dry.
3. Use a potato ricer to the mashed the potato.
4. Get a large mixing bowl: Add the potato with 1 tbsp of butter. Allow the butter to melt slightly from the heat of the potato.
5. Add the flour and mix them well. Stir in the egg with a pinch of salt then combine them well to make the dough.
6. Transfer the mix into a floured surface and knead it with your hands for 12 min until it becomes soft.
7. Divide the dough into 16 pieces and rolls each of them into 3 1/2 inches circle.
8. Put a plum in the middle of each dumpling circle and wrap it around it to make a ball then place it on a greased baking sheet with the sealed side facing down.
9. Repeat the process with the remaining ingredients.
10. Place a large pot of water over medium heat with a pinch of salt. Lower into it some dumplings and cook them until they float on top while stirring them gently.

11. Drain the dumplings and coat them with the crumbs then serve them with your favorite sauce.
12. Enjoy.

PEACH STUFFED
Potato Dumplings

Prep Time: 2 hrs
Total Time: 2 hrs 20 mins

Servings per Recipe: 10
Calories	761 kcal
Fat	19.2 g
Carbohydrates	135.3g
Protein	12.6 g
Cholesterol	43 mg
Sodium	225 mg

Ingredients

8 potatoes - peeled and cubed
1 egg
5 C. all-purpose flour
10 firm ripe peaches
1 C. white sugar

1/2 C. butter, melted
1 (16 oz) package vanilla wafers, crushed

Directions

1. Bring a salted pot of water to a boil. Add the potato and cook it until it becomes soft. Remove it from the water.
2. Get a large mixing bowl: Use a potato ricer to mash the potato and place it in it. Add the egg and flour. Mix them well until you get a soft dough.
3. Place the dough aside to rest for 2 min. Cut the dough in half in spread each one on a floured working surface until it becomes 1/4 inch thick.
4. Cut the dough into squares according to the size of the peaches. Place each peach in the middle of a square and wrap it around it then pinch it to seal it.
5. Repeat the process with the remaining ingredients. Bring a large pot of water to a boil then cook in it the dumplings in batches until they float to the top.
6. Transfer your dumplings into a serving plate and slice them in half. Discard the peach pit then drizzle over them some melted butter, vanilla wafers and sugar.
7. Serve your dumplings right away hot with some ice cream.
8. Enjoy.

Fruity
Dumplings Flour

🥣 Prep Time: 20 mins
🕐 Total Time: 3 hrs 50 mins

Servings per Recipe: 8

Calories	672 kcal
Fat	15.8 g
Carbohydrates	124.6 g
Protein	11.2 g
Cholesterol	34 mg
Sodium	960 mg

Ingredients

4 C. self-rising flour
1 3/4 C. dried currants
1 2/3 C. raisins
1/4 lb shredded suet
1 C. dry bread crumbs
1 C. white sugar
1 egg, lightly beaten

1/2 C. milk
1 tsp mixed spice
1 tsp baking powder
1 pinch salt
1 tbsp molasses

Directions

1. Place a large pot of water over medium to high heat. Cook it until it starts boiling.
2. Get a large mixing bowl: Add the flour, currants, raisins, suet, bread crumbs and sugar. Stir them well.
3. Get a medium mixing bowl: Whisk in it the egg and milk with mixed spice, baking powder, salt and molasses. Transfer the mix to the flour mix. Combine them well until your get a smooth dough.
4. Dip a large heavy cotton piece of cloth in the pot with the boiling water. Drain it and sprinkle some flour all over it.
5. Place the dough in the middle of the cloth and pull on it corners to the side. Fold the cloth on top and tie with a kitchen twine.
6. Place it in the pot with boiling water. Lower the heat and let it cook for 3 h 32 min. Drain the dumpling and place it in front of a heated oven until it dries completely.
7. Serve it with your favorite gravy, stew or sauce.
8. Enjoy.

SHORTENING
Dumplings

Prep Time: 20 mins
Total Time: 1 hr 20 mins

Servings per Recipe: 5
Calories   250 kcal
Fat   8.2 g
Carbohydrates   38.2g
Protein   5.2 g
Cholesterol   0 mg
Sodium   466 mg

Ingredients

2 C. all-purpose flour
3 tbsp shortening
1 tsp salt

1/4 C. water

Directions

1. Get a large mixing bowl: Stir in it the flour with salt. Add the shortening and mix them until they becomes crumbled.
2. Add the water and mix them again until you get a soft dough. Place it on a working surface and spread it. Cut the dough into 1 inch wide strips.
3. Fill a large saucepan with broth and bring it to boil. Cook in it the dumplings for 12 min. Put on the lid and cook the for another 12 min.
4. Serve your dumplings with some that broth hot and chicken, beef or meat.
5. Enjoy.

Steaks

Gravy with Dumplings

🥣 Prep Time: 20 mins
🕐 Total Time: 2 hrs 5 mins

Servings per Recipe: 6	
Calories	445 kcal
Fat	17.6 g
Carbohydrates	37.3g
Protein	32.5 g
Cholesterol	131 mg
Sodium	1541 mg

Ingredients

2 tbsp vegetable oil
1 1/2 lb beef round steak, cut into 1/4-inch thick strips
1 tbsp garlic powder
1 tsp salt, or to taste
1 tsp ground black pepper, or to taste
1 (14 oz) can beef broth
1/2 onion, diced
1 C. chopped carrot

3 cubes beef bouillon
2 C. all-purpose flour
1 tsp salt
1/4 tsp baking powder
2 eggs, beaten
3/4 C. water, or as needed

Directions

1. Place a large pan over medium heat. Heat the oil in it. Add the steaks strips with garlic powder, a pinch of salt and pepper. Cook the for 14 min while stirring all the time.
2. Stir in the broth and scrap the brown bites then add the onion with carrot, bouillon cubes. Cook the stew until it start simmering.
3. Lower the heat and cook them for 1 h 32 min the steak is done.
4. When the steak gravy is almost done, start making the dumplings.
5. Place a large pot filled with water and pinch of salt over medium high heat and bring it to a boil.
6. Get a large mixing bowl: Mix in it the flour, 1 tsp of salt, and baking powder. Add the egg followed by the water gradually while mixing all the time until you get a sticky dough.
7. Spoon the dough in the size of dumplings to the boiling top. Cook them until they rise to the top. Drain them and sere them hot with the steak gravy.
8. Enjoy.

QUICK
Dumplings

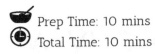 Prep Time: 10 mins

Total Time: 10 mins

Servings per Recipe: 6
Calories   173 kcal
Fat   1.2 g
Carbohydrates   34.1g
Protein   5.6 g
Cholesterol   3 mg
Sodium   568 mg

Ingredients

2 C. all-purpose flour
2 tsp baking powder
1 tsp salt

1 C. milk

Directions

1. Get a large mixing bowl: Stir in it the flour with baking powder and a pinch of salt. Add the mix gradually while whisking all the time until the dough becomes soft.
2. Cook the dumplings the way you desire.
3. Enjoy.

Italian
Herbs Dumplings

🥣 Prep Time: 5 mins
🕐 Total Time: 20 mins

Servings per Recipe: 6

Calories	182 kcal
Fat	6.7 g
Carbohydrates	25.9 g
Protein	4.4 g
Cholesterol	18 mg
Sodium	772 mg

Ingredients

1 1/2 C. all-purpose flour
1 tsp salt
1 tsp baking soda
2 tsp baking powder
1 tsp dried thyme
1 tsp dried parsley

1 tsp dried oregano
3 tbsp butter
3/4 C. milk

Directions

1. Get a large mixing bowl: Stir in it the flour, salt, baking soda, baking powder, thyme, parsley, and oregano. Add the butter and mix them until they become crumbled.
2. Drizzle the milk gradually while mixing all the time until you get a smooth dough.
3. Spoon the dumplings and drop them on your soup, stew or broth. Put on the lid and cook them for 17 min. Serve them warm.
4. Enjoy.

CROUTONS
Dumplings

Prep Time: 30 mins
Total Time: 50 mins

Servings per Recipe: 8
Calories	136 kcal
Fat	0.9 g
Carbohydrates	28.3g
Protein	3.8 g
Cholesterol	23 mg
Sodium	211 mg

Ingredients

2 large potatoes, peeled and chopped
1 C. self-rising flour
1 egg

8 large seasoned croutons

Directions

1. Place a large pot of water and a pinch of salt over medium high heat. Cook it until it starts boiling. Cook in it the potato until it becomes soft.

2. Get a large mixing bowl: Mash the potato and add 2 C. of it to the bowl with the egg and flour. Mix them well.

3. Shape 1/4 to 1/2 C. of the dough into dumplings. Place a crouton in the middle of each dumpling and wrap the dough around it.

4. Lower the dumplings into the boiling water. Put on the lid and cook them for 22 min. Drain them and serve them warm.

5. Enjoy.

Stuffed Dumplings with Edamame Cream

Prep Time: 15 mins
Total Time: 1 hr 15 mins

Servings per Recipe: 16
Calories	213 kcal
Fat	7.5 g
Carbohydrates	28.3g
Protein	8.2 g
Cholesterol	7 mg
Sodium	686 mg

Ingredients

1 (1 lb) package frozen edamame (green soybeans), thawed
1/4 C. water
1/4 C. olive oil
1/2 C. sour cream
1 tsp salt
1 tsp ground black pepper
1 green onion, chopped
1 clove garlic, chopped

1 tsp fresh lemon juice
1 dash hot sauce
2 (12 oz) packages small won ton wrappers
6 C. water
4 cubes chicken bouillon

Directions

1. Place a large pot of water over medium heat with a pinch of salt. Cook in it the edamame for 12 min. Transfer to an ice bath stop it from cooking. Drain it.
2. Get a food processor: Add edamame and turn on the machine on low. Add to it 1/4 C. of water and oil gradually. Process them until they becomes smooth.
3. Add the sour cream, salt, pepper, green onion, garlic, lemon juice, and hot sauce. Blend them smooth to make the filling.
4. Place a won ton wrapper on a working surface and place 1 tsp of the filling in the middle of it. Pinch 2 of the opposite corners of the wrappers to seal them in the middle.
5. Do the same of the remaining 2 corners using some water to help seal them.
6. Place a large deep pan over medium heat. Combine in it 6 C. water and the bouillon cubes. Cook them until they start boiling.
7. Place the wrapper dumplings in the boiling water and cook them on batches for 6 min until they becomes soft.
8. Serve your dumplings with their cooking broth. Serve them hot.
9. Enjoy.

PARSLEY
Dumplings

Prep Time: 10 mins
Total Time: 1 hr 10 mins

Servings per Recipe: 8
Calories	128 kcal
Fat	1.1 g
Carbohydrates	24.4g
Protein	4.5 g
Cholesterol	23 mg
Sodium	258 mg

Ingredients

2 C. all-purpose flour
1/2 tsp baking powder
1/2 tsp salt
3/4 C. chicken broth
1 egg, lightly beaten

1 tbsp dried parsley
2 tbsp minced onion

Directions

1. Get a large mixing bowl: Stir in it the flour, baking powder, and salt.
2. Get a medium bowl: Mix in it the broth, egg, parsley, and onion. Add the mix to the flour mix and mix them until they make a soft dough.
3. Place the dough on a floured surface and knead it with your hands until it becomes soft. Spread it until it becomes 1/8 inch thick.
4. Add it to your broth, stew or soup. Put on the lid and cook them for 17 min over medium heat. Serve them warm.
5. Enjoy.

Beef Flavored
Liver Dumplings

Prep Time: 30 mins
Total Time: 1 hr

Servings per Recipe: 4
Calories	280 kcal
Fat	7.1 g
Carbohydrates	19.5g
Protein	32.3 g
Cholesterol	359 mg
Sodium	1877 mg

Ingredients

1 lb raw liver
2 C. fresh bread crumbs
1 egg
1/4 C. all-purpose flour
1 dash salt, divided
ground black pepper to taste

2 quarts boiling beef broth

Directions

1. Pour the broth in a large pot and bring it to a boil.
2. Get a food processor: Place in it the liver and process it until it becomes smooth. Add the rest of the ingredients and blend them smooth.
3. Coat a spoon with some water and drop it in the boiling broth. Cook it for 28 min. Serve it hot.
4. Enjoy.

THANKSGIVING
Turkey Leftovers Dumplings

Prep Time: 15 mins
Total Time: 1 hr 10 mins

Servings per Recipe: 10
Calories	194 kcal
Fat	6.9 g
Carbohydrates	16.3g
Protein	15.8 g
Cholesterol	35 mg
Sodium	367 mg

Ingredients

1 lb cooked, chopped turkey meat
3 C. water
salt and pepper to taste
3 tbsp all-purpose flour

1 (12 oz) package refrigerated biscuit dough

Directions

1. Place a large saucepan over medium heat. Add the water with turkey, a pinch of salt and pepper. Cook them until they start boiling.
2. Lower the heat and simmer them for 38 min.
3. Sprinkle the flour over a working surface. Lay on it the biscuits and cut them into 1/2 inch pieces.
4. Drop the dumplings into the hot turkey broth. Put on the lid and lower heat. Cook them for 17 min. Serve your dumpling soup hot.
5. Enjoy.

Stuffed
Cheesy Tuna Dumplings

🥣 Prep Time: 10 mins
🕐 Total Time: 40 mins

Servings per Recipe: 6

Calories	333 kcal
Fat	16.5 g
Carbohydrates	27.8g
Protein	17.6 g
Cholesterol	86 mg
Sodium	844 mg

Ingredients

1 (5 oz) can tuna, drained
1 egg
1 tsp dried parsley
1/2 C. shredded Cheddar cheese
1/2 tsp salt
1/2 tsp ground black pepper
1 (10.75 oz) can condensed cream of broccoli soup
1 (12 fluid oz) can evaporated milk

2 tsp chopped pimento
1 (8 oz) package refrigerated crescent rolls

Directions

1. Before you do anything preheat the oven to 375 F.
2. Get a mixing bowl: Add the egg, parsley, cheese, tuna, a pinch of salt and pepper. Mix them well.
3. Get a small mixing bowl: Whisk in it the soup, milk, and pimentos.
4. Lay a crescent roll on a working surface. Drop a some of tuna filling in the middle of it and fold it. Seal the edges with some water. Repeat the process with the rest of the ingredients.
5. Place the stuffed dumplings in greased baking dish. Pour the milk and soup all over them. Cook them in the oven for 32 min. Serve your dumplings hot.
6. Enjoy.

APPLE PIE
Dumplings

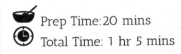 Prep Time: 20 mins
Total Time: 1 hr 5 mins

Servings per Recipe: 16	
Calories	333 kcal
Fat	19 g
Carbohydrates	38.5g
Protein	2.7 g
Cholesterol	31 mg
Sodium	360 mg

Ingredients

2 large Granny Smith apples, peeled and cored
2 (10 oz) cans refrigerated crescent roll dough
1 C. butter

1 1/2 C. white sugar
1 tsp ground cinnamon
1 (12 fluid oz) can or bottle Mountain Dew (TM)

Directions

1. Before you do anything preheat the oven to 350 F. Coat a casserole dish with some oil.
2. Slice the apple into 8 wedges and place them aside. Lay a crescent roll on a working surface. Place an apple wedge at its small end and roll it.
3. Seal it and place it in the casserole dish with the sealed side facing down. Repeat the process with the rest of the ingredients.
4. Place a heavy saucepan over medium heat. Heat the butter in it until it melts. Add the cinnamon with sugar and stir them slightly.
5. Drizzle the mix all over the dumplings followed by the mountain dew. Cook them dumplings in the oven for 42 min. Serve them hot.
6. Enjoy.

Granny's
Vanilla Apple Dumplings

🥣 Prep Time: 30 mins
🕐 Total Time: 1 hr 30 mins

Servings per Recipe: 6	
Calories	899 kcal
Fat	35.4 g
Carbohydrates	147.8g
Protein	4.5 g
Cholesterol	41 mg
Sodium	434 mg

Ingredients

1 recipe pastry for double-crust pie
6 large Granny Smith apples, peeled and cored
1/2 C. butter
3/4 C. brown sugar
1 tsp ground cinnamon

1/2 tsp ground allspice
3 C. water
2 C. white sugar
1 tsp vanilla extract

Directions

1. Before you do anything preheat the oven to 400 F. Coat a casserole dish with some butter or oil.
2. Lay the pastry on a floured surface and cut it into 6 squares. Put an apple on each triangle with the cored side facing up.
3. Slice 8 pieces from the butter and reserve the remaining of it. Place each one in the open side of each apple. Sprinkle the brown sugar over the apples followed by the allspice and cinnamon.
4. Moist your fingers with some water then bring the opposite corners of each square on top of the apple then pinch them to seal them.
5. Transfer the apple dumplings to the greased baking dish.
6. Place a heavy saucepan over medium heat. Add the water, white sugar, vanilla extract and reserved butte. Cook them until they start boiling. Keep them boiling for 6 min.
7. Pour the mix all over the apple dumplings. Cook them in the oven for 1 h. Serve them with some ice cream.
8. Enjoy.

CITRUS
Granny Apple Dumplings

Prep Time: 15 mins
Total Time: 1 hr

Servings per Recipe: 8
Calories	513 kcal
Fat	29.3 g
Carbohydrates	59.1g
Protein	4.4 g
Cholesterol	46 mg
Sodium	570 mg

Ingredients

3/4 C. butter
1 C. white sugar
1 tsp ground cinnamon
1 tsp vanilla extract
1 (12 fluid oz) can or bottle caffeinated citrus-flavored soda

4 small Granny Smith apple, peeled, cored, and quartered
2 (8 oz) packages refrigerated crescent roll dough

Directions

1. Before you do anything preheat the oven to 350 F. Coat a casserole dish with some butter.
2. Place a heavy saucepan over medium heat. Add the butter, sugar, cinnamon, and vanilla. Cook them for 6 min. Turn off the heat and place the syrup aside.
3. Lay the dough on a working surface and divide into 16 triangles. Place a quarter of apple on each dough triangle and roll them.
4. Transfer the apple dumplings into the greased casserole dish. Drizzle the vanilla butter all over it followed by the soda.
5. Cook it in the oven for 47 min. Serve your dumplings warm.
6. Enjoy.

Dublin Dumplings

Prep Time: 30 mins
Total Time: 4 hrs 30 mins

Servings per Recipe: 6
Calories	595 kcal
Fat	9.2 g
Carbohydrates	94.4g
Protein	33.9 g
Cholesterol	58 mg
Sodium	2402 mg

Ingredients

2 (10.75 oz) cans condensed cream of chicken soup
3 C. water
1 C. chopped celery
2 onions, quartered
1 tsp salt
1/2 tsp poultry seasoning
1/2 tsp ground black pepper
4 skinless, boneless chicken breast halves

5 carrots, sliced
1 (10 oz) package frozen green peas
4 potatoes, quartered
3 C. baking mix
1 1/3 C. milk

Directions

1. Place a large pot over medium heat. Stir in it the soup, water, chicken, celery, onion, salt, poultry seasoning, and pepper. Put on the lid and cook them for 1 h 35 min over low heat.
2. Stir in the carrot with potato. Put on the lid and simmer them for 35 min.
3. Drain the chicken from the soup and shred it. Stir the chicken with pea back into the pot. Cook them for 6 min.
4. Get a mixing bowl: Mix in it the baking mix with milk and a pinch of salt until they make a soft dough. Spoon the dough over the stew.
5. Put on the lid and cook the stew for 1 h 40 min over low heat. Serve your stew hot.
6. Enjoy.

CREAMY
Chicken Thighs Soup with Dumplings

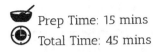

Prep Time: 15 mins
Total Time: 45 mins

Servings per Recipe: 6
Calories   376 kcal
Fat   18.3 g
Carbohydrates   31.4g
Protein   20.8 g
Cholesterol   68 mg
Sodium   1377 mg

Ingredients

6 boneless chicken thighs
2 (10.75 oz) cans condensed cream of celery soup
salt and pepper to taste

1 (12 oz) package refrigerated biscuit dough

Directions

1. Place a large salted pot of water over medium high heat. Add the chicken thighs and cover them with water. Cook them for 22 min.

2. Remove the chicken thighs from the water. Place 3 C. of cooking water aside. Shred the chicken thighs and place them back in the empty pot.

3. Stir in the soup with a pinch of salt and pepper. Lower the heat and dump the biscuits over them. Put on the lid and cook them for 12 min.

4. Serve your dumplings soup hot.

5. Enjoy.

Orangy Apple Dumplings

Prep Time: 15 mins
Total Time: 45 mins

Servings per Recipe: 8
Calories	315 kcal
Fat	17.6 g
Carbohydrates	37.4g
Protein	2.4 g
Cholesterol	31 mg
Sodium	302 mg

Ingredients

2 Granny Smith apples - peeled, cored and quartered
1 (8 oz) can refrigerated crescent rolls
1/8 tsp ground cinnamon
1/2 C. butter

3/4 C. white sugar
1 C. orange juice
1 tsp vanilla extract

Directions

1. Before you do anything preheat the oven to 350 F. Coat a casserole dish with some butter.
2. Lay the crescent rolls over a floured surface. Place an apple quarter over each crescent roll and roll them.
3. Transfer the rolls into the casserole dish and top them with cinnamon.
4. Place a heavy saucepan over medium heat. Add the butter, sugar, and orange juice. Cook them until they start boiling.
5. Add the vanilla extract and stir them. Pour the mix all over the crescent rolls. Cook them in the oven for 35 min. Serve your rolls warm.
6. Enjoy.

CREAMY
Corn and Chicken Dumplings Stew

Prep Time: 25 mins
Total Time: 1 hr 25 mins

Servings per Recipe: 8

Calories	533 kcal
Fat	31.7 g
Carbohydrates	33.4g
Protein	28.9 g
Cholesterol	118 mg
Sodium	1476 mg

Ingredients

3 tbsp butter
2 lb chicken thighs
8 slices turkey bacon
2 stalks celery, chopped
3 carrots, chopped
1 red onion, finely chopped
3 cloves garlic, finely chopped
1 (14 oz) can vegetable broth
1/2 tsp paprika

1/2 C. heavy cream
1 (26 oz) can condensed cream of chicken soup
1 C. water
1 (8.75 oz) can sweet corn, drained
ground black pepper to taste
1 (10 oz) can buttermilk biscuits

Directions

1. Place a large pan over medium heat. Add the butter and melt it. Cook it in the chicken thighs for 8 min on each side. Drain them and place them aside to lose heat completely.
2. Shred the chicken thighs and place them aside.
3. Add the bacon to another pan. Cook them until they become crisp. Drain and place them aside. Break the bacon into crumbs and place them aside. Place 1 tbsp of the bacon grease aside.
4. Heat leftover chicken drippings in a large pot. Add the celery, carrots, red onion, and garlic. Cook them for 6 min.
5. Stir in the chicken with broth and the reserved bacon grease. Cook them for 14 min.
6. Add the paprika, heavy cream, cream of chicken soup, and water. Cook them for 7 min. Stir in the ground pepper with corn.
7. Cut the biscuits into quarters and place them on the stew. Lower the heat and cook them stew and dumplings for 12 min while stirring them gently.
8. Serve your stew and dumplings hot. Enjoy.

Cinnamon
Apple Dumplings

Prep Time: 20 mins
Total Time: 1 hr 5 mins

Servings per Recipe: 12

Calories	406 kcal
Fat	19.6 g
Carbohydrates	57g
Protein	3.5 g
Cholesterol	31 mg
Sodium	288 mg

Ingredients

3 lb apples - peeled, cored and sliced
2 C. all-purpose flour
1 1/2 C. white sugar
2 tsp baking powder
1 tsp salt

2 eggs, beaten
1 C. vegetable oil
1 tsp ground cinnamon

Directions

1. Before you do anything preheat the oven to 350 F. Coat a casserole dish with some butter.
2. Get a large mixing bowl: Mix in it the flour, sugar, baking powder, and salt. Add the eggs and oil then mix them again.
3. Lay the apple slices in the greased baking dish. Spread the dough over it and top it with cinnamon.
4. Cook it in the oven for 44 min. Serve your dumplings warm.
5. Enjoy.

CHICKEN BREASTS
Stew with Milk Dumplings

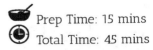

Prep Time: 15 mins
Total Time: 45 mins

Servings per Recipe: 6
Calories	310 kcal
Fat	9.4 g
Carbohydrates	35.4g
Protein	20.1 g
Cholesterol	45 mg
Sodium	1362 mg

Ingredients

1 (32 oz) container chicken broth
4 skinless, boneless chicken breast
halves, cubed, or more as needed
1 onion, chopped
1/2 (16 oz) package baby carrots
2 stalks celery, chopped

1 bay leaf
salt and ground black pepper to taste
2 1/4 C. baking mix
2/3 C. milk

Directions

1. Place a large pot over medium heat. Stir in it the broth, chicken breast cubes, onion, carrots, celery, bay leaf, salt, and pepper.
2. Lower the heat and put on the lid. Cook the stew for 28 min.
3. Get a large mixing bowl: Mix in it the milk with baking mix until they make a dough. Spoon the dough over the stew. Put on the lid and cook them for 12 min.
4. Serve your chicken stew dumplings hot.
5. Enjoy.

Rotisserie
Chicken Stew with Dill Dumplings

Prep Time: 20 mins
Total Time: 1 hr 5 mins

Servings per Recipe: 8
Calories	464 kcal
Fat	21.3 g
Carbohydrates	37.9g
Protein	29.7 g
Cholesterol	96 mg
Sodium	1161 mg

Ingredients

1 (3 lb) rotisserie chicken
2 tbsp butter
1 onion, diced
2 ribs celery, sliced thin
2 tbsp all-purpose flour
2 (14.5 oz) cans chicken broth
1 tsp salt
1/2 tsp ground black pepper
1/2 tsp dried basil
1/4 tsp dried thyme

3/4 lb new potatoes, cut into 1/2-inch dice
2 C. frozen mixed vegetables
1 1/2 C. all-purpose flour
2 tsp baking powder
1/2 tsp salt
3 tbsp butter
3/4 C. milk, or more as needed
2 tbsp dried dill

Directions

1. Shred the rotisserie chicken and place it aside.
2. Place a large soup pot over medium heat. Add 2 tbsp of butter and heat it until it melts.
3. Add the celery with onion and cook them for 12 min. Stir in 2 tbsp of flour then mix them for 3 min while cooking all the time.
4. Add the broth gradually while mixing all the time. Stir in 1 tsp salt, black pepper, basil, thyme, potatoes, and mixed vegetable.
5. Put on the lid and cook the stew for 18 min. Stir in the shredded chicken and leave the stew cooking.
6. Get a large mixing bowl: Combine in it the 1 1/2 C. flour, baking powder, and 1/2 tsp salt. Add the butter and mix them until the mix becomes crumbled.
7. Add the dill with milk. Mix them well until the dough becomes sticky. Spoon the dough over the chicken stew.
8. Put on the lid and cook the stew dumplings for 12 min. Serve it hot.
9. Enjoy.

HEARTY
Creamy Chicken Soup with Dumplings

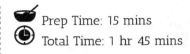

Prep Time: 15 mins
Total Time: 1 hr 45 mins

Servings per Recipe: 6
Calories	750 kcal
Fat	34.4 g
Carbohydrates	57.7g
Protein	49.5 g
Cholesterol	132 mg
Sodium	2206 mg

Ingredients

2 tbsp butter
1 onion, diced
3 large bone-in chicken breast halves with skin
1 (32 oz) can chicken broth
3 C. all-purpose flour
1 tbsp baking powder
1 1/2 tsp salt
1/3 C. vegetable shortening, plus

2 tbsp vegetable shortening
3/4 C. milk
1 (10.75 oz) can condensed cream of chicken soup
2 C. water
1/2 tsp salt
1/4 tsp ground black pepper

Directions

1. Place a large soup pot over medium heat. Add the butter and heat it until it melts. Add the onion and cook it for 6 min.
2. Add the chicken with broth and water to cover the chicken. Cook the soup over high heat until it starts simmering. Lower the heat and put on the lid.
3. Cook the soup for 1 h 5 min. Drain the chicken breasts and shred them. Stir them back into the pot. Keep the soup simmering.
4. Get a large mixing bowl: Combine in it the flour, baking powder, and 1 1/2 tsp of salt. Add the vegetable shortening and mix them with your hands until the mix becomes crumbly.
5. Add the milk gradually while mixing all the time. Transfer the dough into a floured working surface and knead it with your hands until the dough becomes soft.
6. Slice the dough into 12 dumplings and place them aside. Add the chicken soup with 2 C. water, salt, pepper to the soup. Cook the soup until it starts simmering.
7. Place the dumplings on top. Put on the lid and lower heat. Cook the soup and dumplings for 15 to 22 min or until the dumplings float on top.
8. Serve your chicken soup and dumplings hot. Enjoy.

Twice Stuffed Dumplings

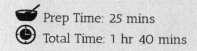

Prep Time: 25 mins
Total Time: 1 hr 40 mins

Servings per Recipe: 12
Calories	253 kcal
Fat	10.6 g
Carbohydrates	33.2g
Protein	6.4 g
Cholesterol	68 mg
Sodium	698 mg

Ingredients

Sauerkraut Filling:
2 tbsp butter
1/3 C. chopped onion
1 1/2 C. sauerkraut, drained and minced
salt and pepper to taste
Potato Filling:
3 tbsp butter
1/2 C. chopped onion
2 C. cold mashed potatoes

1 tsp salt
1 tsp white pepper
Dough:
3 egg
1 (8 oz) container sour cream
3 C. all-purpose flour
1/4 tsp salt
1 tbsp baking powder

Directions

1. To make the sauerkraut filling:
2. Place a large pan over medium heat. Heat the butter in it until it melts. Add the onion and cook it for 4 min.
3. Add the sauerkraut with a pinch of salt and pepper. Cook them for 6 min. Place the filling aside to lose heat completely.
4. To make the potato filling:
5. Place a large pan over medium heat. Heat the butter in it until it melts. Add the onion and cook it for 6 min.
6. Stir in the potato with a pinch of salt and pepper. Cook it for 3 min. Place the filling aside.
7. To make the dumplings:
8. get a large mixing bowl: Add the sour cream with eggs. Mix them well. Add the flour, salt, and baking powder. Mix them well until your get a dough.
9. Place the dough on a floured surface and knead it until it becomes soft. Slice the dough in half and roll each one until it becomes 1/8 thick.
10. Cut the dough into 3 inches circles. Divide the potato filling on the circles by placing them

in the middles and pinch them to seal them then place them aside.

11. Repeat the process with the remaining filling and circles.

12. Place a large pot of water over medium heat. Fill it with water and cook it until it starts boiling.

13. Cook the dumplings in the boiling water and cook them until they float on top. Drain them and serve them warm.

14. Enjoy.

Turkey Stew
with Buttermilk Dumplings

Prep Time: 10 mins
Total Time: 4 hrs 10 mins

Servings per Recipe: 4
Calories   449 kcal
Fat   22.4 g
Carbohydrates   38.2g
Protein   23.3 g
Cholesterol   70 mg
Sodium   1961 mg

Ingredients

2 (10.75 oz) cans condensed cream of chicken soup
1 (15 oz) can chicken broth
1 1/2 C. chopped cooked turkey, or more to taste
1 C. chopped potatoes, or more to taste
1 C. chopped carrots, or more to taste
1/2 onion, chopped

2 tbsp butter
1 pinch garlic powder
1 pinch poultry seasoning
1/2 (10 oz) can refrigerated buttermilk biscuit dough, cut into squares

Directions

1. Grease a slow cooker: Stir in it the cream of chicken soup, chicken broth, turkey, potatoes, carrots, onion, butter, garlic powder, and poultry seasoning.

2. Put on the lid and cook the stew for 3 h on high. Dump the biscuits on top of the stew. Put on the lid and cook them for 1 h on high.

3. Serve your stew warm.

4. Enjoy.

CREAMY
Allspice Chicken Stew with Dumplings

Prep Time: 30 mins
Total Time: 3 hrs 30 mins

Servings per Recipe: 8
Calories	704 kcal
Fat	34.4 g
Carbohydrates	53.1g
Protein	42.5 g
Cholesterol	224 mg
Sodium	1542 mg

Ingredients

1 (3 lb) whole chicken
1 onion, chopped
1 stalk celery, with leaves
1 tbsp poultry seasoning
1 tsp whole allspice
1 tsp dried basil
1/2 tsp salt
1 tsp black pepper
1 tsp seasoning salt
1 (10.75 oz) can condensed cream of chicken soup (optional)

Dumplings:
4 eggs
2 tbsp olive oil
1 tbsp salt
1 tsp black pepper
2 C. water
4 C. all-purpose flour

Directions

1. Place a large pot over medium heat. Add the onion with celery and chicken.
2. Cover them with water then stir in the poultry seasoning, whole allspice, basil, 1/2 tsp salt, 1 tsp pepper, and seasoning salt.
3. Cook the stew until it starts boiling. Lower the heat and cook them for 3 h. Drain the chicken and place it aside.
4. Pour the broth through a sieve and strain it. Pour the broth back into the pot and add the chicken soup. Keep the soup simmering.
5. Get a mixing bowl: Add the eggs, olive oil, 1 tbsp salt, and 1 tsp pepper with 2 C. water. Combine in the flour wile mixing them gradually.
6. Pull the dough into several pieces and dump them in the hot broth. Stir them gently. Put on the lid and cook them for 17 min.
7. Shred the chicken and stir it into the pot. Serve your stew hot.
8. Enjoy.

Caramelized Apple Dumplings

Prep Time: 20 mins
Total Time: 1 hr 40 mins

Servings per Recipe: 8
Calories   550 kcal
Fat   21.7 g
Carbohydrates   85g
Protein   6.1 g
Cholesterol   23 mg
Sodium   659 mg

Ingredients

3 C. sifted all-purpose flour
4 tsp baking powder
1 tsp salt
3 tbsp white sugar
1/2 C. shortening
1 C. milk
4 apples - peeled, cored and halved
1/2 C. white sugar

1 tsp ground cinnamon
1/8 tsp ground allspice
3/4 C. packed brown sugar
1/3 C. butter
1 pinch salt
2 C. boiling water

Directions

1. Before you do anything preheat the oven to 375 F. Coat a casserole dish with some butter.
2. Get a small mixing bowl: Add 1/2 C. of the white sugar with the ground cinnamon and the ground allspice. Mix them well.
3. Get a large mixing bowl: Mix in it the flour, add baking powder, salt, and 3 tbsp sugar. Add the shortening and mix them until they become crumbled.
4. Combine in the milk gradually while mixing all the time. Transfer the dough to a floured surface and cut it in half.
5. Roll in each half until it becomes 1/8 thick. Cut the dough into 5 inches squares to make 8 in total. Place half an apple on each square with the open side facing up. Sprinkle 1 tbsp of the sugar mix over each apple half.
6. Cross the corners of the dough squares on top to cover the apple halves completely then pinch them to seal them. Lay the apple halves in the greased casserole dish and place them aside.
7. Place a heavy saucepan over medium heat. Stir in it the brown sugar, butter, salt, and water. Cook them until they start boiling. Pour the mix all over the dumplings.
8. Cook them in the oven for 48 min. Serve your dumplings warm with some ice cream. Enjoy.

THANKSGIVING
Stew with Stuffing Dumplings

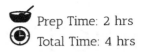

Prep Time: 2 hrs
Total Time: 4 hrs

Servings per Recipe: 12	
Calories	512 kcal
Fat	24.5 g
Carbohydrates	61g
Protein	15.5 g
Cholesterol	43 mg
Sodium	865 mg

Ingredients

1 roast turkey carcass
6 quarts water
4 medium onions
6 medium carrots
5 stalks celery
6 C. leftover stuffing
6 egg whites
cooking spray
1 C. peas
1 C. corn kernels
1 C. cubed turnips

1 C. fresh green beans, trimmed
1 (16 oz) can jellied cranberry sauce
1 (16 oz) can whole berry cranberry sauce
1 tbsp poultry seasoning, such as Bell's
salt and pepper to taste

Directions

1. Preheat the oven broiler. Place the rack away from the heat 6 inches.
2. Separate the meat from the bones of the turkey and place it aside. Place the bones in a roasting dish and cook them in the oven until they well browned.
3. Place a large pot over medium heat. Fill it with 6 quarts of water. peel the onions with celery and carrot then chop them. place them aside and reserve the peel.
4. Add the peel of the veggies with the browned carcass to the pot. Cook them for 1 h 10 min to make the broth. Remove the pot from the heat and allow it to sit for 25 min.
5. Pour the broth in a large fine sieve and strain it. Pour the broth in a large container and place it in the fridge for an overnight. Skim the fat from it every once in a while.
6. Get a large mixing bowl: Add the leftover stuffing with an egg white. Mix them well and shape them mix into dumplings.
7. Lay the dumplings on a heatproof plate and microwave them for 2 min 30 sec.
8. Place a large pan over medium heat. Grease it with a cooking spray. Brown in it the

dumplings until they become golden brown then place them aside.

9. Pour the broth into a large soup pot. Add the chopped veggies with shredded turkey. Cook the soup for 1 h 10 min.

10. Add the peas, corn, green beans, and turnips. Cook the soup for 14 to 18 min until the veggies becomes soft.

11. Stir in the jellied sauce and whole berry cranberry sauces, poultry seasoning, a pinch of salt, and pepper. Cook them while stirring for 6 min.

12. Add the dumplings and cook the soup for 6 min. Serve it hot.

13. Enjoy.

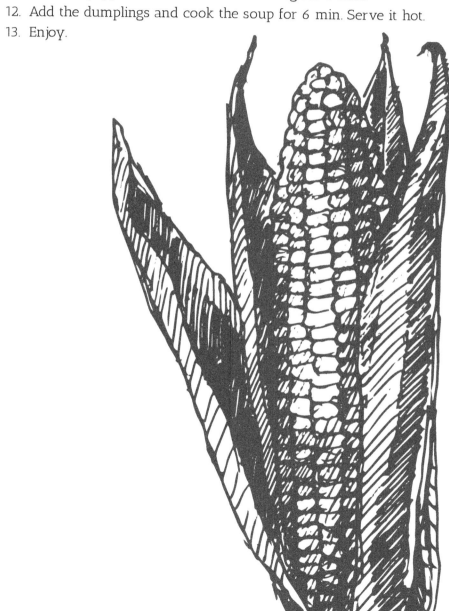

MAPLE
Blueberry and Apple Dumplings

Prep Time: 1 hr
Total Time: 1 hr 45 mins

Servings per Recipe: 6
Calories	444 kcal
Fat	16.8 g
Carbohydrates	70.2g
Protein	6.1 g
Cholesterol	43 mg
Sodium	488 mg

Ingredients

2 C. all-purpose flour
1 tbsp baking powder
1/2 tsp salt
2 tbsp brown sugar
1/2 C. butter, chilled and diced
3/4 C. milk
6 apples, peeled and cored
1 C. blueberries

1/4 C. maple syrup
1 tsp ground cinnamon
1/2 tsp ground allspice
1 tsp dried orange peel

Directions

1. Before you do anything preheat the oven to 400 F. Coat a casserole dish with some butter.
2. Get a large mixing bowl: flour, baking powder, salt and brown sugar. Add the butter and mix them until they become crumbled.
3. Add the milk gradually while mixing all the time until you get a smooth dough. Knead the dough on a floured surface and knead it until it becomes soft.
4. Cut the dumplings into 6 inches squares to make 6 of them.
5. Put an apple in the middle of a square and fill its core with blueberries. Pour some maple syrup all over it. Pull each 2 opposite corners on top and pinch them to seal them.
6. Lay the fruit dumplings in the greased baking dish then top them with allspice and cinnamon.
7. Get a mixing bowl: Whisk in it the rest of the maple syrup with enough water to cover 1 inch of the pan. Pour the mix all over the dumplings.
8. Scatter on top the orange peel with the apple peel and any leftover berries.
9. Cook them in the oven for 48 min while pouring the basting them with the liquid all over them. Serve them hot.
10. Enjoy.

Jarlsberg's
Dumplings Casserole

Prep Time: 30 mins
Total Time: 1 hr 15 mins

Servings per Recipe: 6
Calories	373 kcal
Fat	20.7 g
Carbohydrates	34.2g
Protein	12.9 g
Cholesterol	121 mg
Sodium	1019 mg

Ingredients

2 C. mashed potatoes
1 C. all-purpose flour
2 eggs, beaten
1 1/2 tsp salt
1/8 tsp black pepper
1 medium onion, chopped
3 tbsp butter
2 tbsp all-purpose flour

1 C. light cream
1 C. chicken broth
1/2 C. grated Parmesan cheese
1/2 C. shredded Jarlsberg cheese

Directions

1. Get a large mixing bowl: Add the mashed potatoes, 1 C. flour, eggs, salt and pepper. Mix them well.
2. Bring a salted pot of water to a boil. Spoon the dough in dumplings into the hot water. Cook them until they float on top.
3. Drain the dumplings and place them in a greased baking dish. Place it aside.
4. Before you do anything preheat the oven to 350 F.
5. Place a large pan over medium heat. Cook in it the butter until it melts. Add the onion and cook it for 3 min.
6. Stir in the four and cook them for 1 min. Add the cream with broth. Cook them while stirring all the time until the mix becomes thick.
7. Add the parmesan cheese with half of the jarlsberg cheese. Drizzle the mix all over the dumplings. Top them with the remaining cheese.
8. Cook them in the oven for 48 min. Serve your dumplings casserole hot.
9. Enjoy.

FRENCH
Milk Dumplings

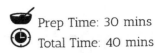

Prep Time: 30 mins
Total Time: 40 mins

Servings per Recipe: 4
Calories   506 kcal
Fat   12.3 g
Carbohydrates   78.8g
Protein   20.5 g
Cholesterol   113 mg
Sodium   1220 mg

Ingredients

1 (1 lb) loaf stale French bread, cut into
1 inch cubes
1 C. milk
2 tbsp butter
1 onion, finely chopped
1 tbsp chopped fresh parsley
2 eggs
1/2 tsp salt

1 pinch ground black pepper
1/2 C. dry bread crumbs (optional)

Directions

1. Place a heavy saucepan over medium heat. Cook in it the milk until it starts bubbling.
2. Get a large mixing bowl: Place in it the bread and cover it with the hot milk. Allow the mix to sit for 16 min.
3. Place a large pan over medium heat. Add the butter and cook it until it melts. Cook in it the onion for 4 min. Add the parsley and turn off the heat.
4. Transfer the mix to the milk and bread mix with the eggs, salt and pepper. Mix them with your hands until you get a sticky dough.
5. Fill a large pot with water and a pinch of salt. Cook it over medium to high heat until it starts boiling.
6. Moisten your hands with some water and shape some of the mix into a dumpling. Place it in the boiling water. If it held itself repeat the process with the rest of the dumplings.
7. Cook them until they float on top for about 22 min. If the dumpling crumbled add some breadcrumbs to the mix and try another one.
8. Serve your dumplings warm.
9. Enjoy.

Asian
Stuffed Shrimp Dumplings

Prep Time: 50 mins
Total Time: 1 hr 5 mins

Servings per Recipe: 12
Calories	411 kcal
Fat	22.3 g
Carbohydrates	16.1g
Protein	34.5 g
Cholesterol	152 mg
Sodium	454 mg

Ingredients

1 lb raw shrimp, peeled and deveined
4 lb ground beef
1 tbsp minced fresh ginger root
1 shallot, minced
1 bunch green onions, chopped
3 leaves napa cabbage, chopped
2 tbsp soy sauce
1 tsp Asian (toasted) sesame oil

salt and white pepper to taste
1 pinch white sugar
1 (10 oz) package round gyoza/potsticker wrappers
vegetable oil
1/4 C. water

Directions

1. Get a food processor: Add the shrimp and process it until it becomes smooth. Place it aside. Repeat the process with the beef.
2. Get a large mixing bowl: Add the shrimp with beef, ginger, shallot, green onions, napa cabbage, soy sauce, sesame oil, salt and pepper, and white sugar.
3. Combine them well to make the filling. Place it aside.
4. Lay a wrapper on a working place. Put a scant tsp of the filling in the middle then wrap it and use some water to seal it.
5. Pace a large pan with a lid over medium heat. Heat the oil in it. Add the some of the stuffed wrappers with the sealed side facing down.
6. Cook them for 2 to 3 min until they become golden brown. Flip them and cook them the same way on the other side. Place all the dumplings as once in the pan and pour the water all over them.
7. Put on the lid and cook them for 3 to 4 min or until the water evaporates. Serve your dumplings warm.
8. Enjoy.

PRUNE STUFFED
Potato Dumplings

Prep Time: 35 mins
Total Time: 2 hrs 55 mins

Servings per Recipe: 12
Calories	326 kcal
Fat	10.4 g
Carbohydrates	53g
Protein	6.8 g
Cholesterol	54 mg
Sodium	243 mg

Ingredients

4 large russet potatoes
1/2 tsp salt
1 tbsp butter, softened
2 eggs, beaten
1/4 C. farina
1 C. all-purpose flour, or as needed
12 Italian prune plums
12 cubes white sugar

1/2 C. butter, melted
1/4 C. white sugar
1 C. dry bread crumbs
additional melted butter and sugar for garnish (optional)

Directions

1. Bring a large salted pot of water to a boil. Cook in it the potato until it becomes soft. Drain the potato and peel it. Place it aside to cool down. Mash it.
2. Get a large mixing bowl: Combine the mashed potato with salt, egg, and 1 tbsp of butter. Mix them well. Add in the farina followed by flour gradually while mixing all the time.
3. Transfer the to a floured working surface and knead it with your hands until it becomes soft.
4. Slice the plums open and discard their pits then replace them with the sugar cubes.
5. Spread the dough until it becomes 1/4 inch thick. Slice into 3 inches squares to make 12 of them.
6. Put each plum in the centre of a squared and pull both the opposite corners of the dough to seal them and cover the plum.
7. Place a large pot of water over medium to high heat and cook it until it starts boiling. Lay in it some of the dumplings and cook them until they rise to the top.
8. Keep them cooking for an extra 6 min. Drain them and place them aside.
9. Place a small pan over medium heat. Add 1/2 C. of butter and cook it until it melts. Add the bread crumbs, and 1/4 C. of sugar. Cook them until the breadcrumbs becomes brown.

10. Drain them and place them aside. Toss the dumplings gently in the melted butter mix in the pan until they are all coated with it.

11. Garnish your dumplings with the breadcrumbs then serve them.

12. Enjoy.

VANILLA
Raisins Dumplings

Prep Time: 15 mins
Total Time: 4 hrs 15 mins

Servings per Recipe: 20	
Calories	487 kcal
Fat	10.5 g
Carbohydrates	92.5g
Protein	7.7 g
Cholesterol	16 mg
Sodium	308 mg

Ingredients

8 C. all-purpose flour
1 C. white sugar
2 tbsp baking powder
1 tsp salt
1 (15 oz) package raisins
1 1/2 (12 fluid oz) cans evaporated milk

2 C. dark molasses
1 tsp vanilla extract
3/4 C. butter, melted

Directions

1. Get a large mixing bowl: Add the flour, sugar, baking powder, salt, and raisins. Mix them well. Place it aside. Add the butter and mix them until they become crumbled.
2. Get a small mixing bowl: Whisk in it the milk, molasses, and vanilla extract. Add it to the flour mix and mix them until you get a dough.
3. Place a large pot of water and fill it with water. Lower into it a heatproof plate. Cook the water until it starts boiling.
4. Place the dough in the middle of a large piece of cotton cloth. Pull the dough to the sides. Tie its tip with a kitchen twice leaving enough space of it to rise.
5. Place the dough in the hot water. Put on the lid and cook them again until they start boiling. Lower the heat and cook them for 3 h 35 min.
6. Drain the dumpling from the water and discard the cloth. Place the dumping to dry then serve it.
7. Enjoy.

Seafood
Stuffed Dumplings

🥣 Prep Time: 40 mins
🕐 Total Time: 1 hr

Servings per Recipe: 6
Calories	373 kcal
Fat	17.7 g
Carbohydrates	37g
Protein	17.4 g
Cholesterol	43 mg
Sodium	1579 mg

Ingredients

1 C. frozen shelled edamame (green soybeans)
1/3 lb large shrimp - peeled, deveined, and cut into 1/3-inch pieces
1/2 C. finely chopped bok choy
1 egg white
1 tbsp minced fresh ginger root
1 tbsp soy sauce
1 tbsp sesame oil
1 clove garlic, minced, or more to taste
1 tsp salt
2 tbsp water
36 dumpling wrappers
1/4 C. peanut oil, divided
1 C. water, divided
1/2 C. low-sodium soy sauce
1 tbsp sesame oil
1 green onion, sliced
2 tsp white sugar
1 tbsp rice vinegar
1/2 tsp red pepper flakes, or to taste

Directions

1. Steam the edamame for 5 min.
2. Get a food processor: Place in it the edamame and process it until it becomes smooth.
3. Get a large mixing bowl: Mix in it the edamame with shrimp, bok choy, egg white, ginger, soy sauce, 1 tbsp sesame oil, garlic, and salt.
4. Place a wrapper on a working surface. Place 1 tsp on the side of it and moisten its edges with some water. Pull the other side over the filling and pinch the edges to seal them.
5. Place a large pan over medium heat. Heat 1 tbsp of peanut oil in it. Add the dumplings and cook them in batches for 2 to 3 min on each side.
6. Place all the dumplings in the same pan. Pour 1/4 C. of water on them. Put on the lid and cook them until the water completely evaporates.
7. Get a small mixing bowl: Whisk in it the low-sodium soy sauce, sesame oil, green onion, sugar, rice vinegar, and red pepper flakes to make the sauce. Serve your dumplings with the sauce. Enjoy.

CREAMY
Paprika Chicken with Parsley Dumplings

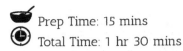

Prep Time: 15 mins
Total Time: 1 hr 30 mins

Servings per Recipe: 8	
Calories	525 kcal
Fat	28.2 g
Carbohydrates	38.5g
Protein	28.4 g
Cholesterol	77 mg
Sodium	1736 mg

Ingredients

3 tbsp vegetable shortening
1 C. all-purpose baking mix
2 tsp salt
1 tsp paprika
1/8 tsp ground black pepper
2 1/2 lb bone-in chicken parts
2 (10.5 oz) cans cream of chicken soup, undiluted

3 C. milk
Dumplings:
2 C. all-purpose baking mix
2/3 C. milk
1/2 tsp dried parsley
1/4 tsp poultry seasoning

Directions

1. Place a large pan over medium heat. Add the shortening and melt it in it.
2. Get a mixing bowl: Mix in it 1 C. baking mix, salt, paprika, and pepper. Dust the chicken pieces in the mix and cook them in the oil for 5 to 7 min on each side. Place it aside.
3. Combine the soup with milk in a clean pan. Cook them until they start boiling. Lower the heat and add the chicken pieces.
4. Put on the lid and cook them for 47 min while stirring them from time to time.
5. Get a large mixing bowl: Add 2 C. baking mix, milk, parsley, and poultry seasoning. Mix them well until you get a smooth dough.
6. Spoon the dough over the cooked chicken and place the dumplings on top. Cook them for 12 min. Put on the lid and cook them for another 12 min.
7. Serve your chicken dumplings hot.
8. Enjoy.

Chili
Dumpling Sauce

Prep Time: 10 mins
Total Time: 1 hr 10 mins

Servings per Recipe: 10
Calories	6 kcal
Fat	0.4 g
Carbohydrates	0.7g
Protein	0 g
Cholesterol	0 mg
Sodium	538 mg

Ingredients

3 tbsp light soy sauce
3 tbsp dark soy sauce
3 tbsp balsamic vinegar
1 tsp hot chili oil
1 tsp minced fresh ginger root

1/2 tsp white sugar
1 clove garlic, chopped
1/4 tsp minced green onion, or to taste

Directions

1. Get a small mixing bowl: Add all the ingredients and whisk them well. Pour the sauce in a container and place it in the fridge for 1 h.

2. Enjoy.

SESAME
Feta Stuffed Dumplings

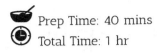

Prep Time: 40 mins
Total Time: 1 hr

Servings per Recipe: 20
Calories	210 kcal
Fat	12.4 g
Carbohydrates	19.3g
Protein	5.5 g
Cholesterol	62 mg
Sodium	346 mg

Ingredients

3 1/2 C. all-purpose flour
2 tsp baking powder
1/2 C. canola oil
1/4 C. butter, melted
1 C. plain yogurt
3 beaten eggs
1 tbsp sour cream
1 tbsp white sugar

1 1/2 tsp salt
1 C. crumbled feta cheese
1 C. finely chopped fresh parsley
1 tbsp olive oil
2 tsp paprika
2 egg yolks
2 tbsp sesame seeds

Directions

1. Before you do anything preheat the oven to 375 F. Cover a baking pan with a piece of parchment paper.
2. Get a mixing bowl: Stir in it the flour with baking soda.
3. Get a large mixing bowl: Place in it the canola oil, butter, yogurt, eggs, sour cream, sugar, and salt. Combine them well.
4. Add the flour mix and stir them until you get a smooth dough. Place the dough on a floured surface and knead it until it becomes soft.
5. Get a small mixing bowl: Mix in it the feta cheese, parsley, olive oil, and paprika to make the filling.
6. Shape the dough into 2 1/2 tbsp balls and press them until they become 3 inches wide.
7. Put 1 scant tbsp of filling in the middle of circles. Pinch the corners on top then seal them with some water. Place the dumplings in the baking sheet.
8. Get a small mixing bowl: Add the eggs yolks and beat them slightly. Brush the dumplings with the beaten egg yolks then top them with the sesame seeds.
9. Cook them in the oven for 28 min. Serve them warm.
10. Enjoy.

Italian
Tomato Soup with Buttermilk Dumplings

Prep Time: 30 mins
Total Time: 1 hr

Servings per Recipe: 4
Calories	229 kcal
Fat	6.8 g
Carbohydrates	36.3g
Protein	8.8 g
Cholesterol	9 mg
Sodium	1771 mg

Ingredients

Soup:
1 tbsp olive oil
1/2 yellow onion, roughly chopped
2 cloves garlic, minced
1 tsp dried Italian seasoning
1 (28 oz) can crushed tomatoes
2 C. water, divided
2 tsp salt
Dumplings:
3/4 C. all-purpose flour
1 tsp baking powder

1/4 tsp salt
1/4 tsp freshly cracked black pepper, plus more to taste
1/4 C. shredded sharp Cheddar cheese
1/2 C. buttermilk, shaken
2 tbsp chopped fresh Italian parsley
Reynolds Wrap(R) Aluminum Foil

Directions

1. Before you do anything preheat the oven to 350 F.
2. Place an oven heatproof pot over medium heat. Heat the oil in it. Add the onion and cook it for 4 min.
3. Stir in the garlic and Italian seasoning. Cook them for 1 min. Add the tomato with 1 C. of water. Cook them until they start simmering.
4. Lower the heat and simmer the soup for 16 min. Get a food processor or blender then blend the soup until it becomes smooth in batches.
5. Pour the soup back into the pot. Add more water if it is too thick. Bring it to a simmer.
6. Get a large mixing bowl: Add the flour, baking powder, salt, black pepper, and cheese. Add the buttermilk gradually while mixing all the time until you get a dough.
7. Spoon the dough dumplings into the pot with the hot soup. Place it in the oven and cook it for 24 min. Serve it warm.
8. Enjoy.

BEGINNERS'
Creamy Chicken Stew with Bisquick Dumplings

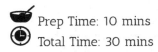

Prep Time: 10 mins
Total Time: 30 mins

Servings per Recipe: 4
Calories   340 kcal
Fat   13.8 g
Carbohydrates   33.8g
Protein   20.6 g
Cholesterol   45 mg
Sodium   1069 mg

Ingredients

1 1/2 C. milk
1 C. frozen green peas and carrots
1 C. cut-up cooked chicken
1 (10.75 oz) can condensed cream of chicken mushroom soup

1 C. Original Bisquick(R) mix
1/3 C. milk
Paprika, if desired

Directions

1. Place a large saucepan over medium heat. Add the 1 1/2 C. milk, the peas and carrots, chicken and soup. Cook them until they start boiling while stirring all the time.

2. Get a mixing bowl: Add the Bisquick mix and 1/3 C. milk. Mix them until you get a soft dough.

3. Divide the dough into 8 dumplings and place them over the chicken stew. Cook them for 12 min. Put on the lid and cook them for an extra 12 min. Serve them hot.

4. Enjoy.

Garlicky
Semolina Dumplings

Prep Time: 10 mins
Total Time: 15 mins

Servings per Recipe: 4
Calories	96 kcal
Fat	4.8 g
Carbohydrates	9.8g
Protein	3.3 g
Cholesterol	46 mg
Sodium	18 mg

Ingredients

5 tbsp semolina flour
1/4 tsp garlic powder
1/4 tsp Italian seasoning
1 egg

1 tbsp olive oil
1 pinch salt

Directions

1. Place a large pot over high heat. Fill it with water. Cook it until it starts boiling.
2. Get a mixing bowl: Mix in it the semolina flour, garlic powder, and Italian seasoning.
3. Get a large mixing bowl: Combine in it the egg, olive oil, and salt. Mix them well. Add the flour mix and mix them again until they make a smooth dough.
4. Spoon the dumplings into the hot water. Cook them until they rise to the top. Keep cooking them for 5 min. Serve them right away.
5. Enjoy.

TURKISH
Yogurt Dumplings

Prep Time: 35 mins

Total Time: 1 hr 30 mins

Servings per Recipe: 4	
Calories	560 kcal
Fat	23.2 g
Carbohydrates	64.4g
Protein	23.2 g
Cholesterol	120 mg
Sodium	401 mg

Ingredients

2 C. flour
1/2 tsp salt
2 eggs
1/2 tsp water, or as needed
2 onions, peeled
1/2 lb ground beef

salt and pepper to taste
3 tbsp vegetable oil
1 tbsp red pepper flakes
1 tbsp minced garlic
1 (8 oz) container plain yogurt

Directions

1. Get a small mixing bowl: Stir in it the salt with flour. Combine in the eggs with water. Mix them well until you get a smooth dough while adding more water if the dough is too dry.

2. Cover the dough with a paper towel and place it aside to rest of 35 min. Shred the onion in a press in it in a sieve to remove the water from it. Get a large mixing bowl: Add the onion with beef, a pinch of salt and pepper. Mix them well to make the filling.

3. Split the dough in half. Place one half on a floured working surface and spread it in the shape of a rectangular until it becomes thin. Cut into 2 inches squares. Put 2 tsp of the filling in the middle of each a square and gather its corners on top then seal them with some water.

4. Repeat the process with the rest of the ingredients. Place the finished ones on a floured baking sheet and sprinkle more flour on top of them.

5. Place a small pan over medium heat. Heat the oil with pepper flakes in it until the color of the oil starts changing. Turn off the heat. Place it aside. Get a small mixing bowl: Stir in it the garlic and yogurt to make the sauce. Place it aside.

6. Place a large pot of water over medium heat with a pinch of salt. Cook it until it start boiling. Lower into it some of the dumplings and cook them in batches for 22 min to 27 min.

7. Remove them from the water and place them on serving plates. Drizzle over it the yogurt sauce with the chili oil. Serve them warm. Enjoy.

Mexican
Cheese Dumplings

🥣 Prep Time: 20 mins
🕐 Total Time: 36 mins

Servings per Recipe: 6
Calories	386 kcal
Fat	16.4 g
Carbohydrates	40.2g
Protein	18 g
Cholesterol	50 mg
Sodium	2322 mg

Ingredients

2 links beef sausage, cut into small pieces
1/2 C. part-skim ricotta cheese
1 C. shredded queso asadero (white Mexican cheese)
1/2 C. chopped cilantro
1 clove garlic, finely minced
1/2 tsp cumin
1 tsp salt

1 (14 oz.) package round wonton wrappers
1 tsp olive oil
1 tbsp salt

Directions

1. Heat a large skillet on medium heat and cook the sausage till cooked completely.
2. Remove from the heat and keep aside to cool.
3. In a large bowl, mix together the ricotta, queso asadero, cilantro, garlic, cumin and salt.
4. For the filling in a food processor, add the sausage and pulse till grounded finely.
5. Add the ricotta mixture in the blender and pulse till well combined.
6. Place a tsp of the filling in the center of a wonton wrapper.
7. With a wet finger, moisten the top half edge of the wrapper.
8. Fold in the half and pinch the edges to seal.
9. Repeat with the remaining wrappers and filling.
10. In a pan of the boiling water, add the oil and about 1 tbsp of the salt.
11. Gently place raviolis into the water and cook for about 6 minutes.
12. With a slotted spoon, transfer onto a serving platter.
13. Serve with a topping of the marinara sauce.

Made in the USA
Middletown, DE
17 January 2023

22349195R00031